To Withinfields Primary School.

Enjoy reading together!

from my heart to yours

For Rob, James, Oli and Grace

Acknowledgements

This book is written with love for my husband, Rob, in honour of how we navigate life's adventures together. To my three blessings and my greatest gifts, James, Oli and Grace. You are my inspiration.

To all of the people I have ever met and to all of the people I am yet to meet.

This book is from my heart to yours.

Hello, world

I'm Jo.

It's funny what one day can bring.

You see, one day I had an idea...about a girl with a
big heart, and so here she is, especially for you.

I have had an amazing life so far, full of
adventure and fun, sadness and joy, and
I have met a lot of amazing people along
the way.

In many ways, they are woven into the pages of this book.

I hope you enjoy it.

from my heart to yours

i am delighted to meet you!

Can I share something special with you?

Did you know that life always mirrors the feelings we hold inside?

It's true! We are magical beings!

Would you like to join the girl with a big heart
on her many adventures?

There are ten adventures in total and she meets all kinds of
friends along the way.

The girl with a big heart listens to her thoughts and feelings, and
practises saying honest words in the mirror every day. This makes
her wise and guides her, no matter where she goes, what she does
or who she meets.

I encourage you at the start of each story to take a deep breath in,
listen well and notice what you notice. You will never be wrong.

Are you ready to get started?

Okay then let us begin...

Love, Jo

Contents

i am Happy

Hello, world

I wonder what today will bring.
As I stretch and yawn, I feel my heart sing!

Today is the day I will jump out of bed.
Today is the day there is joy in my head!

I skip to the bathroom to wash my face.
As I look in the mirror, I smile at this honest place.

The mirror you see, is full of the truth.
I feel happy today as I wobble my tooth!

With a spring in my step, I bound down the stairs.
With a happy heart, I tug on my chair!

I eat my breakfast to feed my heart.
With food in my tummy, a walk I will start.

On with my clothes, I dive into my shoes.
I listen to my mind, I have nothing to lose!

I hop to the park, the one near my house.
I give a huge squeal, it's Stanley the mouse!

Stanley shouts angrily, "Hey, watch where you're going!"
His voice is so cold, I think maybe it's snowing!

My heart feels a shudder and I start to frown.
A mouse that is grumpy, soon brings me down.

I now have a choice to make on the spot.
Do I choose to be happy or choose to be not?

The impact I feel on my mood makes me stop.
It's funny how others can make your heart pop.

I choose to be happy and continue my walk.
A bird now swoops by and she's starting to talk.

"What a day I am having," the bird started saying.
"I woke up so angry, the trees started swaying!"

"Tell me," I said, "why do you feel this way?
I woke up quite happy when I started my day."

"My neighbours, you see," the bird was still speaking.
"They started it all by sticking their beaks in!"

"They shouted at me for singing too loud!
"It isn't my fault I was feeling quite proud."

"Well listen to me for a moment," I said.
"It's a choice you see, that thought in your head."

"It's up to you to stay angry all day."
I think I was helping her choose a new way.

"I see," said the bird, tilting her head to one side.
Then a smile appeared as her heart warmed inside.

"It's lovely to meet you, I am called Heather.
"My mum called me something that sounds just like feather."

"I'll choose to be happy for the time I'm awake.
"Then tomorrow I'll see which path I will take."

The bird thanked me kindly and then flew away.
I look at the time and can no longer stay.

"What a day" I thought as I skipped through the park.
"I really must dash before it gets dark."

Back to my house, I was quite hungry you see.
It's funny how one day can shape how you'll be.

The lesson I take from how I'm now feeling, is that nothing
can stop you living the life you believe in.

Only you can change the way that you feel.
I ask for guidance when it becomes a big deal.

Goodbye for now until next time.
I hope you learnt something from my happy rhyme.

I am Sad

Hello, world

I wonder what today will bring.
As I stretch and yawn, I feel a little sadness within.

Today is the day I will crawl out of bed.
Today I sense a dark cloud above my head.

I drag my feet to the bathroom to wash my face.
As I look in the mirror, I see an honest place.

The mirror you see, is full of the truth.
I feel sad today as I wobble my tooth!

With no spring in my step, I flop down the stairs.
With a heavy heart, I tug on my chair.

I eat my breakfast to feed my heart.
Catch sight of my bike, a ride I might start.

A trip outdoors would make me feel better.
Or should I stay home, curled up in my sweater?

"Get some fresh air!" said the voice in my head.
My sad little heart just wanted my bed.

So on with my clothes, I pull up my sock.
I reach for the key and undo my bike lock.

I pedal quite slow and up a big hill.
"Hello, how are you?" came a voice, quite shrill.

Ted the dog came towards me, his tail wagging wildly.
My heart flickered dimly though his face was so kindly.

"You seem to be troubled, my friend," Ted said.
"You're right," I replied, "I just want my snug bed."

"I know how that feels," Ted smiled back at me.
"I can feel like that too, it's quite natural, you see."

Ted was such a good friend and wanted to listen.
By sharing my thoughts something started to glisten.

I realised that sadness was a friend to me too.
It was showing me exactly what I needed to do.

We mustn't stuff down what's there in our heart.
Ted and his kindness were a light in the dark.

Was it an accident I saw Ted today?
Or was it because my heart went astray?

Whatever the reason I didn't quite care.
I felt brighter inside now and lighter than air!

Back to my house, I was quite hungry you see.
It's funny how one day can shape how you'll be.

The lesson I take from how I'm now feeling, is that nothing
can stop you living the life you believe in.

It doesn't matter that at times I feel blue.
Once I accept myself fully, I'll know what to do.

Goodbye for now until next time.
I hope you learnt something from my sad rhyme.

i am Curious

Hello, world

I wonder what today will bring.
As I stretch and yawn, I notice my mind questioning.

Today is the day I will roll out of bed.
Today is the day I'll explore the thoughts in my head!

I wander to the bathroom to wash my face.
As I look in the mirror, I sense an honest place.

The mirror you see, is full of the truth.
I feel curious today as I wobble my tooth!

With a quizzical step, I study the stairs!
With a curious heart, I tug on my chair.

I eat my breakfast to feed my heart.
I think and I ponder, now where shall I start?

I'm not sure what I'll eat to fill up my tummy.
One thing I know is it needs to taste yummy!

I consider my options. What do I love most?
Will it be cereal? Or maybe just toast?

It's such a great thing to question oneself.
As I reach for my bowl, high up on the shelf.

I gaze out of the window at the shape of the clouds.
Will they burst into big raindrops then splash to the ground?

I am in the mood for some fitness, so I decide to run!
A quick sprint through my neighbourhood, now that'll be fun!

I race to my sports gear, stuffed in my drawer.
Now where are my trainers? Ah, yes, they're on the floor.

I leave my house, curious as to who I might see.
Then all of a sudden, I am being chased by a huge bee!

A buzzing and humming sound rings in my ear.
I am sprinting so fast and shaking with fear!

Bees, you see, they are awfully clever.
I knew they could sting, one stung my friend Trevor!

I looked left and then right. I had broken free.
I ran as fast as lightning. Phew, no sting for me!

I was out of breath now and so very thirsty.
Then out of the alleyway purred this cat known as Kirsty!

"Well, you look sweaty," she said whilst glaring.
I wanted to go home now, I was sooooo past caring!

But a question popped up right out of the blue.
"What do cats really love to do?"

"Well now that you ask, I sleep quite a lot!
"I'm choosy you know, I have a favourite spot!"

"It might be in the sunlight or under a warm car.
"I try to stay local. I don't like to go far."

"Oh, I see, that's interesting. I thought you chased mice?"

Kirsty yawned and replied.
"To tell you the truth they don't taste very nice!"

"Well, I've learned a thing or two about cats
and the things that you do.
"If I didn't ask questions, I would not have a clue!"

"Yes, it's fun to keep learning and finding things out."

"I must make my way home, it will be lunchtime, no doubt."

It's often surprising when meeting such cats.
They open your mind to such interesting facts!

Always stay curious and keep your mind growing.
There are trillions of things in this world well-worth knowing!

Back to my house, I was quite hungry you see.
It's funny how one day can shape how you'll be.

The lesson I take from how I'm now feeling, is that nothing can
stop you living the life you believe in.

Goodbye for now until next time.
I hope you learnt something from my curious rhyme.

i am Worried

Hello, world

I wonder what today will bring.
As I stretch and yawn, I feel a worry begin.

Today is the day I will creep out of bed.
Today is the day there is fear in my head!

I tremble to the bathroom to wash my face.
As I look in the mirror, I dread this honest place.

The mirror you see, is full of the truth.
I feel worried today as I wobble my tooth!

With a knot in my tummy, I struggle downstairs.
With a chattering mind, I tug on my chair.

I eat my breakfast to feed my heart.
I feel sick inside. How do I start?

I peek out of the window, the sun is still shining.
So why am I sat here so worried and not smiling?

A worry, you see, can be carried all day.
A worry not shared just won't go away.

Suddenly, there's a knock on my door.
Who could this be? Today, I'm not sure.

I decide to see who it might be.
I feel anxious inside, not the usual me.

"Hello, love!" the squirrel sung with great cheer.
Maybe he'd help me get rid of my fear.

"Why is it that you're looking so glum?"
I could not fake it or even play dumb.

Well, that's what true friends are really for.
The ones who love you and knock on the door.

Andy is so kind without even knowing.
Whilst sitting beside me, my words started flowing.

With all of this worry, I am not sleeping you see.
Andy listened intently, he really cared about me.

Now that I'd shared, my worries were forgotten.
Sleeping tonight would not be so rotten.

Life's golden ticket is a good night's sleep.
Bright-eyed and bushy-tailed, like Andy
I would soon be.

When we close our eyes the day melts away.
As do our worries, they don't tend to stay.

"Thank you, Andy, for sitting with me.
"What is it you called for, what help can I be?"

"When I feel anxious or worried," Andy frowned,
"I write it all down and my day soon turns around."

I listened intently at what he had said.
It's funny what wiggles around in your head!

Andy stood up and hugged me goodbye.
When your worries are shared, time sure does fly by.

Andy then disappeared out into the street.
My heart started warming right down to my feet.

How lucky I am to have such a good buddy.
At a time in the day when my head felt so fuzzy.

The lesson I take from how I'm now feeling, is that
nothing can stop you living the life you believe in.

Goodbye for now until next time.
I hope you learnt something from my worry rhyme.

i am Kind

Hello, world

I wonder what today will bring.
As I stretch and yawn, I feel a tender understanding.

Today is the day I will float out of bed.
Today is the day to wear my compassionate head!

I move softly to the bathroom to wash my face.
As I look in the mirror, I sense an honest place.

The mirror you see, is full of the truth.
I feel kind today as I wobble my tooth!

With a gentle step, I acknowledge the stairs.
With a grateful heart, I tug on my chair.

I eat my breakfast to feed my heart.
I feel like it's time to visit the local park.

Before I get dressed and get ready for giving.
I hear a rumbling inside. I must eat to keep living!

I must always remember before I face others as part of my day,
that I need to take care of me and only I know the right way.

I need to take care of me and the things that I need.
I try and listen to myself in order to succeed.

I feel quite empty this morning and need to fuel up.
So, a banana in my porridge then fresh juice in my cup.

Sometimes it's water and that's more than okay.
Water is a good source for work, rest and play.

With a smile on my face and a glow from inside.
I just know I must visit this fancy new slide.

Right, on with my trainers it's time to go.
I'll lead with my heart, and I'll go with the flow.

I skip down the path, it must have been raining last night.
There are a few wiggly worms that now come into sight!

I feel for these worms, stranded right here.
They need the earth. Oh, there's some here to
bring them cheer!

There you go, Khalid, Carly and Bill.
Off you go now, no need to lay still.

"Why thank you, kind girl," comes a chorus of voices.
I look in the soil so pleased the worms have more choices.

Crawling in gardens and making holes in the ground.
I'm delighted I notice and turn them around.

I'm sure I see tiny smiles appear on their faces.
Who cares if I don't, as they are now in the right places?

"Yooohooooo, girl with hair that's fantastically curly.
"Thanks for saving us. Most people don't care because
we are squirmy!"

"You're welcome. I simply imagined myself in your shoes.
"I could not walk by, it was the kind thing to choose."

Then more worms appeared - Doris, Clive, Uttam and Jim.
My eyes are so dazzled I don't know where to begin!

Out from the ground pop more smiling faces.
"You saved our friends from those dangerous places!"

"After the rainfall we sometimes lose our way
We are grateful to you for saving us today!"

I kneel down beside my collection of new friends.
It's tricky to see where a worm starts and then ends.

One thing for sure is they're glowing inside.
That fills me right up with a huge sense of pride.

"See you soon, take care in the rain,
I'll be sure to keep a look out should I meet you again."

A quick go on that slide before heading home.
Caring for oneself and others means you're never alone.

The lesson I take from how I'm now feeling, is that nothing can
stop you living the life you believe in.

Goodbye for now until next time.
I hope you learnt something from my kind rhyme.

i am Fun

Hello, world

I wonder what today will bring.
As I stretch and yawn, I feel a fun tingling.

Today is the day I will tumble out of bed.
Today is the day there is "hoopla" in my head!

I dance to the bathroom to wash my face.
As I look in the mirror, I laugh at this honest place.

The mirror you see, is full of the truth.
I feel fun today as I wobble my tooth!

With a get set, go, I race down the stairs.
I win first place and I jump on the chair!

I eat my breakfast to feed my heart.
I'm sat on my own so let out a big fart!

I feel all excited and giddy inside.
This ball of fizziness has nowhere to hide!

It pops and it bubbles on the inside of my tummy.
I have a strong feeling that today might be funny!

I quickly get dressed in my bright clothes and wellies.
I dance around my house like a big bowl of jelly!

I'm excited, you see, to get some fresh air.
With adventure in my heart and the breeze through my hair!

I skip down the street with fun in my feet.
Overflowing with sparkle for who I may meet.

Then all of a sudden, I stop on the spot.
It is Stuart, my friend, is he upset or not?

Stuart the hedgehog is usually a prickly fellow.
When I saw him last week though, he had started to mellow.

"Are you okay?" I asked, my heart full of care.
"Why thank you, my dear. You're so sweetly aware.

"At my age," he said, "there is no need to hurry.
But I'm lacking the bubble, the fizz and the flurry!

"I'm feeling a bit low to tell you the truth.
I sometimes miss out on the fun of my youth."

"C'mon, Stuart, age is just a silly number or two.
We can have lots of fun together, just me and you!

"You don't have to be a kid to feel love and connection.
A true friend will always help you flow in the right direction."

A smile started spreading all over Stu's face.
Beaming was changing his speed and his pace.

Just then, a leaflet floated down from the sky.
"A funfair!" I squealed, "let's give it a try!"

Merry-go-round, big dipper and treats.
Bright lights and loud music, such toe-tapping beats!

I looked over at Stuart now full of cheer.
Choosing to have fun together was a brilliant idea!

"Some friends just make you feel better
when you're around them," he smiled.
"You're one of those friends, thank you, my dear child."

I gave him a hug and then had to run.
Time sure flies by when you're having such fun!

The lesson, you see, when your friends lose their smiles.
Is to share one of yours as they travel for miles.

Recall the good times and always have fun.
For you are a brilliant human who is second to none!

The lesson I take from how I'm now feeling, is that nothing can
stop you living the life you believe in.

Goodbye for now until next time.
I hope you learnt something from my fun rhyme.

i am Angry

Hello, world

I wonder what today will bring.
As I stretch and yawn, I feel a burning within.

Today is the day I will storm out of bed.
Today is the day there is rage in my head!

I stomp to the bathroom to wash my face.
As I look in the mirror, I grimace at this honest place.

The mirror you see, is full of the truth.
I feel angry today as I wobble my tooth!

96

I don't want any food, I don't want to go outside.
I want to stay under my duvet all day and just hide.

With a crash and a bang, I slip on the stairs.
Now fuming with pain, I kick my own chair!

"Oh typical!" I yell, all cross and quite mad.
I knew it, I thought, that today would turn bad!

I slam my bowl down and make quite a din.
Then, out of nowhere, a beautiful butterfly flies in!

"How did you get in here?!" I shout out aloud.
"Never you mind that, I'm here to turn your frown around."

"Well good for you!" I snap at the butterfly.
"I lose my temper easily, I don't have to try!"

I yank open the cupboard to make myself toast.
"Feeling angry," said the butterfly, "is the feeling I struggle with most.

"I see who you are," the butterfly gently lays bare.
"It happens a lot to people who care."

"Whatever do you mean?" I scowl and splutter.
"It's typically when we're hurt," the butterfly flutters.

"Anger, you see, is the bodyguard of pain.
It's just like when my wings feel heavy with rain."

"I realise now what you're saying is true.
Sometimes people are mean to me.
Are they mean to you, too?"

"Of course they are, sweet girl so bright.
In life we must learn to protect our own light.

"I now rise above it, higher than high.
This way I can always reach for the sky."

"Wow, thank you, this makes perfect sense in my head.
Just lift myself up, whenever I see red."

"Don't stuff it down or try to hide.
Allow it to show you and be your true guide."

The butterfly lands on the tip of my nose.
Teaching me that my gut feeling always knows!

"What's your name before you fly from this room?"
"My name? That's easy. My name is June."

"So wonderful to meet you, you're a breath of fresh air.
Be sure to call in again, until then take good care."

My feelings have changed, my anger set free.
Don't stay there too long though, set a firm boundary.

The lesson I take from how I'm now feeling, is that nothing can
stop you living the life you believe in.

Goodbye for now until next time.
I hope you learnt something from my angry rhyme.

i am Embarrassed

Hello, world

I wonder what today will bring.
As I stretch and yawn, I feel unsettled within.

Today is the day I will slink out of bed.
Today is the day there is uncertainty in my head!

I tiptoe to the bathroom to wash my face.
As I look in the mirror, I peek at this honest place.

The mirror you see, is full of the truth.
I feel embarrassed today as I wobble my tooth!

With an awkward step, I attempt the stairs.
With an uneasy heart, I tug on my chair!

I eat my breakfast to feed my heart.
I try to brush off this feeling and make a new start!

I feel like going on an exciting adventure, do you?
Like maybe a swim, the park or the zoo!

You know, the sort of place where kind people care.
Where they consider the planet and animal welfare.

I grab hold of my rucksack, I'll have lunch on the go.
I'm not sure how long my travel will take me,
you don't always know!

I eat a healthy breakfast and give my body some good stuff.
If I do not eat properly, my day will be tough.

I reach for the sugar, I fancy something quite sweet.
Chocolate and cake are yummy, but just for a treat!

On with my clothes, my wellies and my rucksack.
I throw in some fruit as I like a good snack!

I jump on the bus, hoping for an adventurous ride.
"One ticket to the zoo please. Can you park right outside?"

"Outside, you say," said a kind friendly face.
"I'll see what I can do once we get nearer the place."

I continue to look out of the window whilst dreaming.
I catch sight of myself, and my face is now beaming.

"Wildlife zoo!" I hear a voice say.
"Thanks for the ride. I hope you have a nice day!"

I run through the gate, my ticket in hand.
Oh, WOW how incredible what a magical land!

Just then from a bush in front of a lake.
I hear a strange noise and hope it isn't a snake!

"Psst!" came a sound as clear as a bell.
Is it behind me? It is tricky to tell.

"It's okay. Don't be bashful, come out and say hello."
"I'm quite shy," said the voice, "I'm Julia, the Flamingo."

As I looked closely, I saw a beautiful colour of bright pink!
"Why would you hide such beauty?" I started to think.

"Is it safe to come out?" Julia said.
"I feel embarrassed sometimes, I know it's all in my head.

"I stay here most of the day, amongst the bushes.
That way no-one can see my bright blushes."

"I understand," I said kindly.
"It's safe to come out, you can stand right behind me."

Julia peeked out, first one foot and then the other.
I had to hold back, I just wanted to hug her!

"It's great to meet you. Your bright feathers are amazing.
Let's go to the lake near the water's edge so you can gaze in!

"Can you see how beautiful and delicate you are?
You could be a ballerina. You really are quite the star!"

"Why thank you so much, I do not feel quite so shy. I feel happy inside
now and believe this is the reason why."

"When you look at yourself and accept who you are, inside and out.
There really is nothing much to feel embarrassed about."

Julia danced on her tiptoes and twirled round and round.
I thought for a moment her legs would get twisted and
she'd fall to the ground!

Then all of a sudden, she started to sing!
Her friends gathered round; they loved what was happening.

"I must go now!" I shouted, above all the singing.
My bus had arrived, I could hear a faint bell ringing.

Julia came up close and waved her wing.
"Come back soon," she said.
"Thank you, you taught me to sing!"

"You could sing all along, you just needed to see."
"I did, my friend, because you truly believed in me!"

I jumped back on the bus, now beaming inside.
It's funny how some friends think they must hide.

I think it's good to know who YOU are.
Accept yourself fully and YOU will go far!

The lesson I take from how I'm now feeling, is that nothing can
stop you living the life you believe in.

Goodbye for now until next time.
I hope you learnt something from my embarrassed rhyme.

I am Creative

Hello, world

I wonder what today will bring.
As I stretch and yawn, I feel a ding-a-ling!

Today is the day I will shimmy out of bed.
Today is the day there is magic in my head!

I cha-cha to the bathroom to wash my face.
As I look in the mirror, I visualise an honest place.

The mirror you see, is full of the truth.
I feel creative today as I wobble my tooth!

With a twirl in my step, I pirouette down the stairs.
With a happy heart, I dance with my chair!

I eat my breakfast to feed my heart.
I place the food on my plate like a fine piece of art!

I feel a swirling and twirling inside of my brain.
A fantastic feeling of imagining; ideas falling and
dancing like rain!

I pretend that my stairs are a boat to a faraway place.
I slide down them with dreams and smiles all over my face!

I imagine my breakfast is a feast full of amazing fruit
and of course a sweet treat!
I imagine wearing silver sparkly shoes upon my two feet!

In my mind I can dress in the most twinkly of clothes.
Sequins of course from my head to my toes!

My imagination, you see, is my one special gift.
It takes me wherever I want to be, like a kind of virtual lift!

I was lost in my own world just then for a while.
I must go to the bathroom and re-check on my smile.

The mirror you see is full of the truth.
I swirl and twirl and wiggle that tooth!

I dress up for my day in my fabulous costume.
I nip to mum's room and borrow some perfume.

I am uncertain today of where I may wander.
Who might I meet? And what might I ponder?

I jump in my carriage drawn by a huge white-winged horse!
(I'm dreaming, you see, it is my bike of course!)

Lost in the moment is where creativity lives.
When I imagine and dream, oh the joy that it gives!

Into the breeze I fly, feeling lighter than air.
My legs pedalling fast, the wind blowing my curly hair!

Around the corner I go like a merry-go-round.
Then down from the sky, a dragonfly falls to the ground!

"Weeeeeeeeeee," came a squeak from this magnificent creature.
"I was testing my wings out; they have this snazzy new feature!"

"Oh fantastic!" I cried. "You are so very courageous."
"Well, you've got to challenge yourself in life, because laziness is contagious!"

"You are joyful and so graceful, what is your name?"

"I am Natasha and it's essential to have a brave heart,
like mine, in this flying game!"

"I'm an artist too, powered by creativity and love.
Sometimes the ideas just fit like a hand in a glove."

"Well, it's a pleasure to meet you on such an exciting day.
Maybe you could fly by my house soon, so we can play?"

"I certainly will, that sounds like good fun.
I'll bring us a treat, maybe a coffee and an iced bun!"

"Well, I must dash now as I have so much to do.
I'm delighted I landed here, right next to you."

I couldn't believe it; a dragonfly so positive and kind!
Once you start imagining, there are so many friends
you can find.

I rode home on my bicycle, my heart full to the top.
When you have lots of magical ideas, it is so hard to stop!

As I walk through my door, my thoughts continue to roam.
Then I remember, there is no place like home!

The lesson I take from how I'm now feeling, is that nothing
can stop you living the life you believe in.

Goodbye for now until next time.
I hope you learnt something from my creative rhyme.

i am Love

Hello, world

I wonder what today will bring.
As I stretch and yawn,
I breathe out and breathe in.

Today is the day I feel peaceful inside.
I do not feel troubled, I have nothing to hide!

I float to the bathroom, like I am flying through air.
I feel calm from my toes to the tips of my curly hair.

The mirror you see holds only the truth.
I notice a gap. Something's missing...MY TOOTH!

It has gone, disappeared, it has fallen clean out!
Making room for new growth is what life's all about!

We grow and we learn if we tune into our heart.
The child then the adult is never too far apart.

Do not lose your spirit in this adventure called life.
Stay alert and awake, as sharp as a knife!

At times or in moments if you ever lose your way.
Look up to the sky, by night or by day.

The universe, you see, is so big and filled with magic.
To blink and miss all of that would be totally tragic!

Keep your feet on the ground but look up to the stars!
Dream big and believe in the bright light that you are.

I hope in my rhymes you can see who you are too.
And realise that being human is amazing like me and you.

I am here always as a wise guide and friend.
Whether your adventure is a straight path, a twist or a bend.

Be your true self, just you, exactly as you are.
Love is all you need to guide you, and you will go far.

Take one last look in the mirror, be it big or small.

Remember, learning to love and accept
YOURSELF truly is the greatest love of all.

Copyright © Jo Smedley 2024

First edition published 2023 by Jo Smedley

The right of Jo Smedley to be identified as the author of this work has been asserted in accordance with the Copyright, Designs and Patents Act 1988.

All rights reserved.

This book and its illustrations may not be reproduced in part or whole in any form or manner without the express permission of the author and illustrator.

Any requests should be directed to thegirlwithabigheartbook@gmail.com